Getting Beyond
"How Are You?"

Getting Beyond "How Are You?"

David Mains and Melissa Mains Timberlake

Copy Editors: Laura Stocks and Barbara Williams
Cover Design: Scott Rattray
Cover Illustration: Robert Bergin

**Library of Congress
Cataloging-in-Publication Data**

Mains, David R.
    Getting beyond "How are you?" / by David Mains, Melissa Mains Timberlake.
        p.   cm.
    ISBN 1-56476-035-9
    1. Interpersonal communication — Religious aspects — Christianity.
    2. Self-disclosure — Religious aspects — Christianity.
    3. Interpersonal relations — Religious aspects — Christianity.
    I. Timberlake, Melissa Mains. II. Title.
BV4597.53.C64M35 1992
158'.2 — dc20   92-23325
                                          CIP

Contents

Dedicated to

Jim and Carolyn Timberlake

for encouraging their son

Douglas

to open his heart

and ask the right questions.

Chapter 1

The Value of Asking Good Questions

Have you ever gone to church, talked with a number of people, but returned home with the strange feeling that you were all alone or uncared for? Maybe you spoke to a dozen individuals, yet you shared nothing of real substance with any of them. You didn't get to know anyone better, and no one made an effort to get close to you.

"How are you?" "You sure look good in that outfit." "Nice day, isn't it?" "Work going well?" "Great to see you again." Talk can be superficial. Though it seems friendly, when all is said and done, there's not much to latch on to. Some people in the congregation might know your name, where you work, or how many kids you have. But few discover the inner you.

Why do so many of us have difficulty getting past surface talk? Most of us long for deeper relationships. But even if we were to spend an entire evening with a group from the church, we still might come away knowing very little about the other people who were there.

What do people talk about? Sports, movies, television, school, recipes, personalities, books, the weather . . . the list goes on. But that's hardly what's important to us.

So, what seems to be the problem? Part of the difficulty has to do with conversational skills. More specifically, most church people aren't adept at asking good questions.

Case in point: you're in church and the minister says, "Would visitors please raise your hands?" In a large congregation, that might involve ten or fifteen people. Then the pastor announces, "We'd like to take a few minutes to get to know one another. Would those of you who are regulars please greet our visitors and make them feel at home?" What happens then? Most likely, the members of the congregation try to be friendly.

But too often the conversation goes nowhere. "You're a visitor?" "Yes." "First time here, huh?" "That's right." "Never been to this church before?" "No." "Good to have you!" "Thank you." Sound too familiar? Such exchanges take place time and time again. We just aren't able to get beyond the old standbys.

Obviously, "Are you a visitor?" could be improved on. Why? Because the person is limited in terms of how he or she can answer. Most likely the response will be, "Yes, I am." That's like asking, "How are you?" Most people will say, "Fine, thanks." Then the exchange dies and another opportunity to get to know someone is gone.

It's much better to work at asking questions that allow the other person to reveal something more significant. For example, if you ask, "Where do you work?" most likely you'll get a quick answer. The conversation won't go anywhere. But, if you add, " . . . and what's something you enjoy about your job?" you open a window that can reveal more about that person.

Granted, it's hard to ask a meaningful question when you only have about thirty seconds to talk to somebody. But everyone should be able to come up with a good question to ask a visitor after the service is dismissed. Rarely does this ever happen, however. Week after week, year after year, some people say the same things over and over. Would you believe it's common to find long-time members in our churches who still feel like nobody really knows them? Sad, isn't it?

I (David) realized this was a problem early on in my ministry. The church I was pastoring was doing well. But another church in Chicago was struggling, and they asked our congregation for help. This church at one time involved 400 members, but the attendance had dropped to about 25 people.

I decided to establish a small group ministry. During the first meeting I introduced myself and told something unique about who I was. I then had the others in the group do the same. The elderly person next to me was the board chairman. He said, "My name is Robert Ditwiler, and I'm a retired mailman." Sitting next to him was the wife of the vice-chairman, who exclaimed, "Oh, Robert, I didn't know that you were a mailman!" This woman had attended that church for many years, and there weren't a lot of people left in the congregation. Still, she didn't know that Robert had worked all his life as a letter carrier.

It's not uncommon to find that people don't know what other members of their church do, much less the problems they might be dealing with. Obviously, if our conversations can't get beyond, "How are you?" it's difficult to learn about each other. And even though not asking good questions is primarily a communication problem, it has serious spiritual ramifications.

If we can't get beyond superficial talk, how will we learn what people's needs are? If we don't ask questions that get to the core of where people are, will we know how to pray for them? How will we know how to serve each other or celebrate the wonderful ways God is working in lives? In fact, when we don't know people very well, we often assume things we shouldn't. Conflicts occur even between Christians when people don't make an effort to understand one another. But again, by using the simple skill of asking good questions we can enhance all our relationships, including those at church!

Part of what life is all about is discovering the uniqueness of each of God's children. Everyone has interesting aspects about them. We call these their "hot buttons." If you're able to tap into people's "hot buttons," you catch a tone of excitement in their voices. They'll start talking with such animation that good questions automatically start popping into your head.

A person's "hot button" may be something as unusual as breeding nightcrawlers. Even if you don't know the slightest thing about nightcrawlers, you can still learn a lot by pursuing the topic. Ask why the person started collecting worms, and you may find out it was a hobby his father enjoyed. If you allow your questions to build upon one another, you may soon uncover topics like family traditions, other important relationships, and childhood memories, not to mention that you'll learn a whole lot more about nightcrawlers than you ever dreamed!

When my husband Doug and I (Melissa) took a church job in Lebanon, Kentucky, the parents wished us luck in getting their kids to open up. As youth workers, we were familiar with the frustrations dads and moms often have in not being able to talk to their teens. But, we figured we were young and "hip," so we wouldn't have any problems.

During the first Sunday of teaching, we said, "All right, kids, what's something new and exciting that's happened to you over the week?" To our surprise, we got a poor response. The students looked at us as if we were talking in a foreign language. Blank stares! Or else they answered with the least revealing thing they could — like informing us that their football team had won that week. Because the next Sunday was no different, we decided we needed to find a better way to motivate these teenagers to talk about themselves.

The following Sunday we told the kids to form a large circle. On Saturday night Doug and I had come up with a number of specific questions to ask the group. "OK, we really do want to get to know you better. So we're going to ask some questions, and we want each of you to have a chance to answer." We started out with simple, nonthreatening ones like, "What's something you have hidden under your bed?" Smirks appeared on their faces and little giggles could be heard from around the room. "A big lint pile!" or "old photographs," they replied. Some of them teased us, saying they had underwear under there. Anyway, it was wonderful to see them at least start to respond with a little emotion.

We progressed to deeper questions like, "What's one thing you have to deal with as far as peer pressure is concerned?" To our surprise they were extremely open about different areas they struggled with. As the question time went on, these young people revealed more and more about themselves.

We finally ended with, "Tell us something you will have to trust God with this next week." They mentioned problems with parents, pressure to do drugs, relationships with boyfriends and girlfriends, exams that were coming up, etc. Finally we said, "All right, we're almost out of time, one last question." "No, keep asking us more!" they begged. "More questions. We want to keep answering them!" They were actually enjoying talking about themselves.

Through the simple technique of asking good questions, we were able to improve our relationship with these young people. It was just a matter of figuring out what the right questions were. The following Sunday, Doug and I had several teens approach us after the lesson. They wanted to talk. One said, "I had a good week with my parents. We only fought once!" Another asked, "Could you pray for me? I have a big test tomorrow."

Once the lines of communication were open, we were able to begin working on deeper relationships. Contrary to popular belief, teens aren't resistant to answering questions. In fact, like most of us, they want people to be interested in them enough to ask good questions and then listen to their responses.

Often adults say they have a hard time talking with teenagers, but they also mention it's difficult for them to speak with elderly people. "I just don't know what to talk about. We're so different. I'm stuck over what to say." That's what's so wonderful about the whole questioning process! Good questions allow new friendships to develop quickly, and in the same way, established relationships deepen.

I (Melissa) have a special friend. Her name is Mrs. Flossie Richardson. I met her at our church in Kentucky. We've spent many hours together over the past year and a half. I'm twenty-seven and she's seventy-four. Even though there's a big difference in our ages, we enjoy a close friendship, and our relationship has certainly grown through the question/answer process.

Mrs. Richardson (Miss Flossie to her former students) is a retired schoolteacher. From our conversations, I've learned things I would never have known if we hadn't taken the time to ask each other questions. She's told me details about teaching in a one-room schoolhouse. Flossie taught first- through eighth-graders, sometimes with as many as fifty-three children in the class! I know she loves birds, reading poetry, and one of her favorite flowers is the violet. She has arthritis in her leg and sometimes struggles with asthma. I've heard her tell the sweet story about how she first met her husband. I know she was married on Christmas Eve. I'm aware that this time of year can be especially hard for her because it's a reminder of the loss of her husband. I've learned how important phone calls are, and that they help her get through her week. And the list goes on.

The other day, Mrs. Richardson and I went out to lunch together. As we sat at the table eating our Kentucky corn bread, she leaned over and whispered, "Some people don't understand that we could have good times together . . . me being so old and you being so young. But I consider us good friends. In fact, I consider us the best of friends!" Through the simple skill of asking good questions, I've established a friendship I will always treasure.

Chapter One Discussion Questions

1. How skilled are you at asking people good questions? Rate yourself on a scale of 1 to 10, 10 being best, and explain the reason for your rating.

2. Name someone at your church who is good at asking people questions. _____ What is a lesson you can learn from this person?

3. Tell about someone you liked better after you got to know more about him/her.

4. The time just after a worship service is not always the best time to have a meaningful conversation. What can you change to overcome the problems of too little time and too many people?

5. What age-group is hardest for you to feel comfortable talking with, and why?

6. What are ways to discover another person's conversation "hot button"?

7. If you have an "unlikely friend" (like Melissa's Miss Flossie), tell how the friendship developed.

16 Getting beyond "How Are You?"

Write down three good questions you could ask
a visitor after a church service.

1.

2.

3.

Chapter 2

Questions That Get beyond the Obvious

Small talk. You hear a lot of it. Not just from junior high kids either. Laughter is usually involved. That's because small talk is an entertaining, nonthreatening form of communication. Sometimes it requires a little skill, a certain amount of verbal repartee. But before long, small talk can get incredibly repetitious.

"What a game last night, huh?" . . . "Can you believe this weather?" . . . "What's new?" . . . "Did you watch the special on TV last night?" . . . "Your hair looks great! Did you get it cut?"

We hear small talk frequently in the media. There are good programs on radio and TV, but unfortunately much of the dialogue is just verbal banter. Conversations don't go anywhere. When they're finished, we don't really think that much about what's been said. But then it does take our minds off the traffic or help us fill time.

Wouldn't it be tragic, however, to live your whole life only to realize it's been filled primarily with meaningless chatter?

How does a person get around this problem of overdosing on small talk? One way is to learn the simple skill of asking good questions. Relationships deepen when we ask one another questions that get beyond the obvious.

You might wonder what makes a question good or bad. If you're hoping to learn something significant about the person with whom you're talking, then here is one important rule to remember: Try to phrase your question so that the listener will have to respond with more than yes or no or a one-word answer. Here's an example of a poor question.

Melissa: "Dad, do you like sports?"

David: "Yes, I'm not a super athlete, but I like sports."

That didn't go very far, did it? A better question would be one that prompts a longer, more in-depth response. Here's an example of a good question. You'll see the difference.

Melissa: "Dad, if you could have free tickets to any event in the city, what would you choose to see, and why?"

David: "Well, Melissa, your first question got me thinking about sports, so I'll say I'd like to see Michael Jordan and the Chicago Bulls play basketball. I saw him play once, and he's absolutely incredible! When he shoots, it seems as though he just hangs in midair!

However, since you said I could pick any event in the city, I'd probably choose to hear the Chicago Symphony. You see, way back in high school I played the baritone in the band. Now, as I get older, music is becoming a renewed interest. So what I would do is go over the season and see if the Symphony is playing Cesar Franck. He's one of the classical composers I remember, and I'd love to hear his *Symphony in D Minor* again. Even though it's hard to get tickets to the Chicago Symphony, that would be a marvelous evening. So, that's my number one choice."

There you have it—a poor question and a much better one. We learn from the good question that David likes sports and would enjoy a second chance to watch Michael Jordan play basketball. We also find out about David's high school years—he informed us that he played baritone in the school band. If given any choice, he would enjoy hearing the Chicago Symphony. And it would be extra special if he could hear them perform Cesar Franck, a composer he first learned about in his high school days.

From this information, Melissa could begin to form numerous follow-up questions like: "What's a good thing that happened or a funny experience you had in the band?" "What else did you participate in during high school, and how has that played a role in who you are today?" "Who influenced you during your high school years, and why?" Limitless questions would be intriguing subjects to pursue. By following up on these topics, we could get into deeper, more revealing discussions.

The phrase "and why?" tagged onto a question enables a person to disclose more about himself or herself. It provides the opportunity to share details that probably wouldn't have been said otherwise. "And why?" is like a key that opens the gate to all sorts of hidden territory. Melissa's "and why?" made David qualify his answer. Basically, she said, "Don't just tell me *what* you would enjoy doing, but also tell me *why.*"

Let's try another bad question/good question example.

David: "Melissa, what does your husband, Doug, do?"

Melissa: "My husband is a youth minister and a seminary student."

David: "You're not going to say anything else?"

Melissa: "Well, when you ask a limited question, you usually get a limited response."

David: "All right, you've made your point. Here's a better question: When you first met your husband, what did you envision him doing as a career someday?"

Melissa: "Actually, no one's ever asked me that before. When I first met Doug, he was a goalie on our college hockey team, and hockey was his life. He had dreams of going on to the pros. I thought that's what he would end up doing. But God led him in a different direction. Doug started getting involved in the theater department at school, and that's how we got to know each other. Our friendship helped him get in touch with spiritual things and, after we got married, God eventually led him to Asbury Seminary, where he became the assistant to the director of dramatic ministries. He's been able to use his theater training by leading a drama tour to various kinds of churches throughout the South.

	Doug also works as a youth minister at a church in Lebanon, Kentucky.
David:	"Amazing. I have a feeling you could go on and on."
Melissa:	"That's what happens when you ask a good question!"

As you can see from these examples, you can learn a lot about someone if you ask a question the person can work with. Once you're given enough information, it's easier to think of follow-up questions that build on one another. And then you're quickly beyond the small talk that so often keeps us from really getting to know one another.

Again, relationships deepen when we learn to ask questions that get beyond the obvious. The problem with many families today is that their role models come from the TV and radio small talk they hear. This personality-centered "fast talk" then starts to characterize their closest relationships. Because of this, people miss out on the matters that are truly important to family members. If only we could learn to ask questions that dig a little deeper, questions that say, "Hey, you're important to me. I want to know what's happening in your life."

With so little time to spend together as families, can we afford to invest it in meaningless small talk? Shouldn't we learn how to get beyond the superficial and discover what's going on inside people's hearts?

Do you remember the story of the Prophet Samuel, looking for a man to replace Saul as king? In the process, he almost overlooked David. First Samuel 16:7 reads, "The Lord does not look at the things man looks at. Man looks at the outward appearance, but the Lord looks at the heart."

It's a person's heart we're trying to uncover when we suggest asking good questions. We want to discover, "What's this person really about? And how can I get God's perspective on him or her?" We want to look beyond the outward appearance, the surface, the obvious, to begin probing more deeply for what's inside that person's heart.

Not only is this a skill we need to learn in our family systems, but it's a quality that needs to be developed in our church families. Too many times when congregations come together their conversations fail to get beyond the superficial. For example, ten or fifteen minutes before a committee meeting begins is a prime time for asking good questions. However, the situation usually is wasted with small talk. Someone may be hurting, but this crucial time for asking questions is lost. Someone may have had a great victory she could share, but no one was prepared to reach beyond the all too normal "chitchat." Maybe someone desperately needed prayer, but nobody could see the hurt inside his heart.

Let's be even more specific. Perhaps a member of your congregation has a spouse with cancer. When someone sees this person at church, a typical question might be, "How are you?" But that sort of inquiry doesn't really allow the other individual to share true feelings. Most likely the response will be, "All right" or "Oh, I'm hanging in there."

But, if you ask a better question, like "Tell me, what was a struggle you faced this week?" or "I've been praying for your husband, but I'm also interested in how you're doing. Can you share a bit of what you're going through?" Usually you'll find people are quite willing to talk. They just need someone to open the conversation up. But it's too risky and too painful for them to speak if they don't get some kind of good lead.

Few people are given the chance to talk about their hurts and heartbreaks. They should be able to. And they deserve to be heard. But first they probably need to be asked a good question.

It's important that we become adept at fully using the precious moments we have with each other. If we do, we will see significant changes taking place within our church families. Trust will grow. Hearts will be touched.

Chapter Two Discussion Questions

1. Can you recognize small talk when you hear it? How?

2. Name three factors that contribute to small talk in your home.

3. What specific changes can you make to improve conversations at your home?

4. Name two factors that contribute to the small talk problem in many churches.

5. Figure out two things you can do that would make your conversations at church more meaningful.

6.   Often there is an overabundance of small talk at work or school. When good relationships do form in these settings, what encourages this?

7.   When someone is answering a question, what clues might let you know that a good follow-up question would be in order?

Change each of these questions to make them better.

1. How's work? (school, etc.)

2. What did you think of the sermon?

3. Everyone in your family OK?

4. Who do you plan to vote for?

5. So, what's new in Peoria? (Edmonds, Hartford, or your hometown)

6. You doing all right?

Chapter 3

Listening Skills

Early in my ministry I (David) worked as associate pastor in a church of about 800 members. The church hired a new senior minister who wanted to get to know his people in a faster way than the usual one-on-one conversations. He put me in charge of organizing what he thought was a brilliant concept: dessert socials! On each occasion I was to invite several single adults and maybe four or five married couples. Here was the perfect opportunity for our new pastor to get to know a number of people each evening. Unfortunately, things didn't turn out exactly as planned.

After some time and energy was spent organizing these events, we held the first gathering. The guests chose their desserts, did a little socializing, and then sat down. The pastor had the rest of the evening to begin developing relationships. He started by telling a little story about himself. It was amusing, and it set a friendly atmosphere. After the first story, he shared another personal anecdote. This led to one more tale, followed by yet another, and still more. In fact, by the time the evening was finished, few people had said anything except for the pastor! His brilliant plan to get to know his church members had backfired.

While preparing for the next social, I prayed that this get-together would be a bit more productive. Maybe our new minister had just been a little nervous about meeting everyone. I was wrong! The second event was a duplicate of the first. He told the same stories with minor variations. When the night was over, he couldn't have named anybody there. He hadn't learned even the basic facts about those people, let alone their personal needs!

The sad thing was that this happened every dessert night. Like many people, this minister enjoyed being "center stage." He was a performer, energized by being in front of people. As long as there was an audience, he could talk and continue talking. He might still be talking if someone hadn't said, "It's getting late! I've got to go to work in the morning."

Though this example is extreme, the same type of scenario unfolds time and again with people who know how to talk but have never learned how to ask questions. These individuals are often so concerned about turning the focus onto themselves that they fail to listen when other people do say something. For example, maybe after church a man says quietly, "My wife is having surgery this week. The doctor suspects she has a tumor." Instead of replying, "Oh, I'm so sorry. That must be terribly difficult," such a person might respond, "Well, that's interesting. You know, I had surgery two years ago when I had my appendix out." People who haven't developed their listening skills don't know how to relate empathetically to another's comments.

Listening is a skill we need to learn in our churches. In too many conversations, we discover people aren't hearing what's being said. Their minds are on other things, or they're wondering, "What will I say next?" But what a difference it makes when someone listens to us intently. That has great healing power. Hurting people experience the gentle compassion of Christ when we listen to them empathetically.

I (Melissa) have had a number of occasions when friends have shared their burdens and griefs with me. Someone was feeling lonely, insecure, or even suicidal. During our conversation, I didn't offer profound advice or grand wisdom. I just said, "I believe I understand how you're feeling. Tell me more if you want; I'll stay and listen." It didn't really matter what I said, but it was important that I listened. At the end of our conversation, a friend might say something like, "Melissa, you don't know how much this has meant to me. Just having someone to talk to helps me make it through these hard times. Thank you so much!" And all I did was listen empathetically.

Just what do we mean by listening empathetically? Certainly it involves wanting to hear what's inside a person's heart. An empathetic listener is committed to focusing body, mind, and soul on the concerns of the speaker. With this attitude, the listener communicates, "You are special. I'm giving you this time because you're worthwhile to me." That kind of attention often results in changed lives.

In Luke 19, Jesus calls Zaccheus out of the sycamore tree. He informs the tax collector that He will be stopping by his house. Obviously, Jesus wants to get to know Zaccheus. Scripture doesn't tell us everything said during their conversation. But it's doubtful Christ spent the time talking nonstop until Zaccheus finally said, "All right, all right! Stop talking already! I can't take any more!" No, most likely Jesus was attentive to Zaccheus' needs.

In Scripture we see that Jesus is wonderful at asking "good" questions. These help Him understand a person's heart and soul. In Zaccheus' case, Christ must have felt great compassion for him. Possibly our Lord said, "Zaccheus, tell Me where you are coming from. Why are you collecting taxes? Does the way people respond to you hurt sometimes?

Help Me understand your pressures." Apparently, Zaccheus was able to unfold his story, knowing that Jesus was listening to his every word. And, because of that visit, Zaccheus' whole household was changed . . . radically.

Christ calls us to follow His example, to reach out to the Zaccheus types around us. And through our empathetic listening, hurting people can experience the gentle compassion of Christ today.

Have you ever talked to someone and had the impression that person wasn't listening to you? What a painful experience! Recently a girlfriend of mine (Melissa) called and asked if I would join her for lunch. She wanted to "catch up"on what was happening in my life. This was exciting for me! I've always treasured friendships that allow me to share my thoughts and feelings.

We met at a restaurant. After a few minutes of conversation, my friend asked, "Melissa, over this past year, what are some of the ways God has pushed you to grow?" Wow! That was a wonderful question! I thought about it for a moment, and then, with great excitement, began to respond.

But, I noticed that my friend's eyes kept looking in another direction. At first I ignored her lack of eye contact and continued answering her question. But the more I disclosed about myself, the more her eyes gazed across the room. Finally, I figured out what had captured her attention. A soap opera was on the restaurant's television set. She was watching TV while I was revealing something personal.

I can still remember how I felt. I was unimportant, uncared for, and foolish for being so vulnerable. A lump rose in my throat. Sure, when I look back on the situation it's easy to see what happened. My friend never meant to hurt me. But at the time, it was hard not to take her actions personally.

Many of you can relate to that experience. You know the loneliness of relationships struggling to get past the superficial. You've felt the pain, the feeling of rejection that occurs when someone doesn't appear to be listening. It's like the classic situation of the woman who needs to talk to her husband at breakfast but isn't able to get through because he's buried behind the newspaper. Time after time we hear of marriages breaking up because people can't talk to each other or they just don't know one another anymore. Would things be different if they had made a greater effort to listen empathetically to each other early in their relationship?

Unfortunately, the newspaper isn't the only obstacle that gets between people. Our words have to compete with the radio and television, phone calls, the doorbell, people who drop by, church activities, kids having to make it to a practice, board meetings, the PTA. . . . In the midst of everyday life, how do we bring about change?

First, we must make a conscious effort to be effective listeners. This skill doesn't come naturally. In order to really understand people, we need to work at listening to them. It is crucial that we put aside a busy schedule and listen long and hard when others make themselves vulnerable.

Next, when we're listening, it is important to view the other person as someone of great value. We need to have a mind-set that says, "It's quite possible I can learn more from this person than he or she can from me."

Recently, when I (David) was traveling, I met a lady who said, "I want you to know I really appreciate 'The Chapel of the Air,' especially since women are a part of your broadcast team." We spent awhile talking, and I asked her a few questions. As her story unfolded, I found out she worked with learning-disabled children in a large public school district. Since I knew very little about this fascinating topic, I learned so much through listening to her. And as we conversed, I got a chance to affirm that what she was doing has great worth in God's kingdom.

At the close of our time together, she said to me, "This has been so meaningful.

Sometimes people at the church don't see what I'm doing as a ministry. I don't sing in the choir, I don't teach Sunday School, or do the normal things that some consider ministry. But this time together has helped me feel confident that what I'm doing is important." How glad I was that I went into the conversation believing I could learn more from her than she could from me.

Another key to effective listening is to occasionally repeat what your conversation partner has said. "This is what I'm hearing you say. See if I got it right." This response not only improves your listening skills, but it helps the other person clarify what he or she wants understood.

When trying to relate better to our secular society, church people would do well to restate what they're hearing. Look, for example, at the Pro-Life/Pro-Choice face-off. It seems both sides are more concerned about attacking than listening. A lot of anger, bitterness, and resentment leaks out during debates. But does it have to be this way?

Imagine what a beautiful thing it would be if one of the parties said, "Stop for a second. Let me see if I can repeat what I've heard you say. I may not agree, but I'm sincerely interested in understanding you. Did I get this right? And tell me again, please, why is it you feel this way?" This might be the most positive response imaginable! It could heal some of the verbal wounds that result from heated disagreements. Yet this mind-set is so uncommon.

As church men and women, we must learn to be better listeners. We need to understand the suffering world in which we're living and communicate to it a compassionate love. We need to hear others with Christ's ears. If we do this, it's quite likely we will see the gentle compassion of Jesus still changing lives.

Chapter Three Discussion Questions

1. Explain the meaning of Proverbs 18:13: "He who answers before listening—that is his folly and his shame."

2. Who is someone you appreciate for consistently being a good listener, and what can you learn from this person?

3. Tell about a time you were hurt because you were not listened to the way you feel you should have been.

4. Finish this sentence: Sometimes I don't listen the way I should when _____ _____ _____ _____ .

5.　Name someone who might be encouraged if you repeated his/her words back to show that you really did hear what was said. When might be a good time to try this?

6.　What time of day do you find it hardest to be a good listener, and what can be done to make improvements?

7.　If everyone at your church were like you in terms of listening skills, would people be heard empathetically or not?

Chapter 4

Questions I Wish Others Would Ask Me

Almost everyone likes to be asked questions. Granted, some people don't appreciate it when you probe too deeply. But for the most part, friends and associates enjoy it when you show an interest in them by asking insightful questions.

But what should you do if you're asking ALL the questions and seldom are asked anything in return? Sometimes people like talking about themselves so much that it's difficult to get them to inquire about you. After a while one-sided conversations get aggravating. Maybe you've noticed!

The truth is most people don't know how to reverse the questioning process. It's as if they have no idea how to ask a good question in return. So what do we do about this problem? If we can't resolve it, our conversations will drain us of any desire to get to know people.

The solution isn't too hard. But first, let's look at some words from the Apostle Paul in 2 Corinthians 6:11-13. "We have spoken freely to you, Corinthians, and opened wide our hearts to you. We are not withholding our affection from you, but you are withholding yours from us. As a fair exchange—I speak as to my children—open wide your hearts also." The apostle is emphasizing the importance of a balanced relationship. Sharing affections can't be all one-sided. Our conversations shouldn't be either; they need to include a fair exchange.

Paul's reference to opening our hearts to one another brings to mind the word *fellowship*. Webster's dictionary defines fellowship as "A mutual association of persons on equal and friendly terms . . . a mutual sharing, as of experience, activity, interest, etc." In order to have that mutual exchange in our conversations, we need to strike a balance between asking other people questions and sharing about ourselves. Maturing in conversation skills involves learning not to settle for a one-way exchange.

The first step in this process is to recognize some false assumptions. Usually, when we're not asked questions in return we assume the other person isn't interested in getting to know us. That often just isn't true!

It took me (Melissa) a long time to realize this. Typically, in my friendships, I assumed the role of the questioner. I was good at this, and it was something I enjoyed. But my conversations did tend to be one-sided. I would do the question-asking, and my friends would open up and talk. They almost never asked me anything in return. At the end of our time together, my friends would say, "Melissa, this has meant so much to me. I always enjoy talking to you!" I also enjoyed our time together, but a part of me sometimes felt empty, dissatisfied, and hurt.

After years of bottling up my frustration, I learned an important lesson through the honesty of a close friend. After dinner one night when she was getting ready to leave, it happened. Like a pouting child, I blurted out, "I'm so frustrated! Do you know we've talked all night and you haven't asked me a single question? We always talk about you! I enjoy that, but when are we going to talk about me?"

My friend was a bit shocked at my outburst. I don't blame her—I was rather shocked myself!

It was an awkward moment. But then she kindly said, "Melissa, I'd love to spend time talking about what's going on in your life. But whenever I ask a question, you quickly respond and then ask me something else. I just figured you were more comfortable asking me questions than talking about yourself. Besides, you ask such marvelous questions, and it's hard for me to come up with any that are as good. Sometimes I just have a hard time knowing what to ask. I'm sorry you're so frustrated because I'm very interested in learning more about you. Our friendship is extremely important to me."

Her words soothed my hurting spirit. I had falsely assumed that since she didn't ask me questions, she didn't care about me. Her honesty helped me see I was wrong. Her words made me realize that she cared deeply about me. But I needed to understand how difficult it was for her to come up with questions to ask me. Asking good questions is not a skill most people have developed. So we mustn't assume others are not interested in us. Instead, we should learn to direct the conversation so it allows a mutual exchange.

Other problems crop up when we are the ones asking all the questions. Sometimes we assume different "roles" that accompany being the questioner. For example, we can take pride in being the "wonderful conversationalist" who knows just how to reach people where they are. Or we might enjoy being seen as a lay counselor who is skilled at helping others get in touch with their problems. Certainly there are times when it is appropriate to fill roles like these. But the problem comes when we fail to understand that fellowship needs to flow two ways. Healthy communication requires a mutual sharing.

It took me (David) years to realize how important it was not only to ask good questions, but to share something about myself as well. During my travels, I meet many people. Someone will pick me up from the airport or drive me to a meeting. Because I'm good at asking questions, I usually get to know a lot about these people. But at first I rarely revealed much about myself.

At the end of these times together people used to say, "David, I was going to ask you all kinds of questions, but we've done nothing but talk about me. I almost feel guilty that I've talked so much. I didn't get to learn anything about you, and when am I going to have a chance like this again?" They enjoyed the time we had together, but somehow they didn't feel it was fair. I believe they realized the mutuality was missing.

Lately I've learned to incorporate this two-way element into our talks. Now I'm finding that people respond differently to our conversations. More recently I've been hearing comments like, "This has been a most meaningful time. I'm so glad we had the opportunity to get to know each other better."

How do we make sure mutual exchanges occur? The first step is to ask yourself, "What do I enjoy talking about?" It's important to figure out what it is you want other people to know about you. Otherwise, someone may ask you about growing tulips, and if that's not your topic of interest, you're stuck!

The best way to come up with interesting topics is to sit down and make a list. This is an important exercise because it helps to clarify and identify your own "hot buttons."

When I (Melissa) first did this, it took a little effort to get started. But by the time I finished the assignment, I was amazed to see how many topics I absolutely loved. Yet most of these were never discussed during my conversations. Here are a few examples of items I put on my list.

1. Drama: This is one of my strongest interest areas. I love it when people ask me how I'm using my dramatic skills. I enjoy talking about the plays I'm directing, the acting I'm doing, or the improvisation troupe I started. And I get excited talking about the potential of drama being used in the church.
2. Youth work: I was hired as a youth minister at my church. I like talking about my job, and more specifically, about strategies in relating to young people.
3. Personal growth: I enjoy being challenged to put into words what I'm learning about myself and how I'm growing in my faith.
4. Relationships: Family and friends are important to me. They teach me a lot about myself, so I seldom get tired of discussing how much these people mean to me.

Everyone's list will be different, but it's important to write one out. By doing this, you'll get a better understanding of what you want others to know about you. There in front of you will be a tangible list of pertinent information regarding who you are and what you enjoy talking about.

As you will see, I (David) came up with a list much different than Melissa's. Here is a sample of the topics I wrote down.

1. The church: I love to talk about the church, how specific congregations are doing, and creative ways the church is becoming strong and relevant.
2. Spiritual awakening: I've had this interest ever since I was a college student and first heard about revivals and their influences. I'm also getting better at knowing when I've talked too much about revival and should let the conversation move on to other matters. It used to be that once I got started there was no stopping me!
3. History: I know this is close to what I just mentioned. But my interest in history involves much more than the religious aspects.
4. Current events: How does what's happening in the nation or the world relate to the present and future reign of Christ? I love to talk about it!

5. Theater and movies: I'm discriminating about what I watch. But I enjoy analyzing productions. I always ask myself, "What made this a good or bad presentation?" This is a relaxing topic for me.

Get started on your list. You will immediately have a better understanding of where you need to direct conversations so mutual sharing can take place. How? Again, there's an easy way to do this.

You don't have to wait to be asked about these topics. Simply drop clues that help reveal who you are. For example, while a conversation is in process you could say, "Are you at all interested in drama? That's a big interest of mine, and I really enjoy talking about it. Right now, I'm in the middle of directing a play. . . ." You help the other person determine what is important to you. Now, the other party may or may not be interested in this subject. But at least he or she is given a chance to establish a two-way conversation.

A second technique is more frontal. If the other person just keeps talking but never asks you anything, say something like, "I've enjoyed listening to you. Now, why don't we talk a bit about current events? That's a topic I'm more informed about. Here are my thoughts on the election."

Either of these techniques move the conversation in a direction where mutual exchange can occur. You're making sure the conversation isn't all one-sided. Knowing how to help this happen brings satisfaction. It allows you to both understand and be understood.

Chapter Four Discussion Questions

1. In your mind, what determines whether a conversation has been good or bad?

2. Is it more common for you to:
    A. Talk most of the time because you're good at it.
    B. See that others talk by drawing them out through questions.
    C. Make sure there's a balance between how much you talk and how much you get others to talk.

3. How do you think Jesus would have answered the previous question? Explain your answer.

4. Like the Apostle Paul and the Corinthians, describe a relationship you've been in that was too one-sided.

5. Are your primary church relationships characterized by a mutual exchange? Why or why not?

6. If you have often had the experience of asking most of the questions in a conversation, whose fault do you think this is?

7. Do you think Christians' conversational skills are better or worse than those of non-Christians? Give reasons for your answer.

Make a list of four topics you would enjoy talking about and why.

1.

2.

3.

4.

Now add to your list three more topics you feel would also be interesting to you.

1.

2.

3.

Write out a way you can transition a conversation into one of your interest areas.

Chapter 5

Asking Questions in the Family

Family systems are under extreme pressures today. Turn on the nightly news, and you'll more than likely hear about the nation's economic struggles. Switch the channel, and you're hit with statistics about schoolchildren who are exposed to the threat of drugs and alcohol. Pick up a newspaper, and you'll read about the alarming number in our society who are sexually promiscuous.

The list of pressures families must contend with seems endless: a lack of positive role models, failure of school systems, struggles of single parent households, continued racial tensions, impoverished communication skills, a growing generation gap, shortage of time in a fast-paced society.... All these stresses and more make it difficult for a family to survive! In today's culture it's imperative for parents to develop a habit of asking their children good questions and listening carefully to their answers.

When our four children were growing up, I (David) established a simple but valuable tradition. Every three months, I took each child out individually for breakfast. The purpose of these meetings was to insure that once each quarter we spent quality time talking together. They got to pick the restaurant. The three boys usually went for McDonald's. Melissa chose a slightly classier place, a pancake house called "The Lazy Lion." But it didn't really matter where we ended up eating. Each of my kids looked forward to his or her special time alone talking with Dad. In my memory, those are moments I will always cherish.

Early in my ministry, I (David) worked for Youth for Christ. The leaders often referred to Luke 2:52: "And Jesus grew in wisdom and stature, and in favor with God and men." This verse mentions four aspects of growth: mental, physical, spiritual, and social. These categories helped me establish a pattern for asking questions during my breakfasts with the kids.

These are important subjects to cover when you talk seriously with your children. Let me show you the way they keep you in touch with how your kids are doing.

Scripture states that Jesus grew in wisdom. I wanted to know how my children were doing in this regard. Between bites of pancakes or Egg McMuffins, I'd ask them: "What classes do you enjoy and which are the most difficult for you? Are you keeping up on your schoolwork? Do you get along with your teacher? How are your grades? What books are you reading? Are you finding time to spend working on your hobbies?"

It was never a problem getting the kids to talk. They loved the individual attention and expected me to ask whatever I wanted. They'd take another bite of food, then tell me about their math class, go into great detail about the explosive volcano being created out of papier-mâché, or keep me updated on the gerbil ready to have babies in the science class. We spent a good amount of time discussing this mental area, and then moved on to the next category.

Jesus also grew in stature — physically. Typical questions here were: "How do you feel about your appearance? Are you exercising? Do you enjoy the sports you're involved in? What about your clothes? Do you have healthy eating patterns?"

It's important for children to feel good about their bodies! Growing up can be difficult, especially in our society where appearance has such an emphasis. Opening up communication lines helped sensitize me to any feelings of insecurity they had.

Then, Jesus grew in favor with God. We'd swallow the last few gulps of orange juice and move on to matters concerning their spiritual growth. Each kid always knew I'd ask, "How are you doing spiritually?" They got so they anticipated the question, and seemed to analyze how they were doing even before our breakfast time. I think this experience with Dad helped each of them become comfortable talking about spiritual things. As they grew, I noticed them often initiating conversations in this area—"Dad, I'm reading through Hebrews, and I was wondering if you could answer some questions for me," or "What do you think about the end times and the Tribulation?"

Other related questions I often asked were: "Are you enjoying church? How is your prayer life? What are you learning in Sunday School? Is there a temptation you need some help with?"

I wanted the kids to be able to answer honestly. So I was sure never to be critical if they mentioned they were struggling. My purpose was not to judge them or give them a grade. Instead, I wanted to gain a better understanding of how I could be more sensitive as a parent.

Then finally, Jesus grew in favor with men—He grew socially. Sample questions that fit this category were: "Who are some of your new friends? What do you like about them? Is there anyone you're having trouble getting along with? Who are some of the lonely kids at school and can you reach out to them? How do you feel about your relationship with your boyfriend or girlfriend?" (This was always a fun topic, and I never sensed they resented me asking about it.)

In fact, when my oldest son, Randall, came home from college, he once said to me, "What's the deal? Don't you get to have breakfast with your dad anymore after you've been off to college?" I was so pleased! He still wanted to go out with me.

When the children were young, this pattern of open communication was established through the questioning process. It continues to be a significant part of the way we relate. Even now, times together are important to my kids.

Are there other ways parents can establish special times for talking with their children? Going out to breakfast on Saturdays isn't the only option. Mealtime at home is a great occasion to ask questions, but it's getting increasingly rare to find families that sit down and eat together consistently. So how do parents carve out time from their busy schedules to ask questions?

Often I (Melissa) hear parents groan about the amount of time they spend just having to drive kids around. Moms feel their lives are wasting away behind the steering wheel. The amount of time driving to and picking up from football practice, piano lessons, play rehearsals, slumber parties, the shopping mall, etc., can be mind-boggling.

However, there's another way of looking at it. Think about it — in the car you have a captive audience! Since you're spending so much time there anyway, why not use it for everyone's advantage? A drive in the car can be a great time to catch up. Sure, there's always the temptation to switch on the radio or go into the "cabdriver's trance." But don't! Take advantage of the opportunity to turn a cumbersome chore into a positive experience.

I (Melissa) learned how to do this when my husband and I were houseparents at a boys' home. With six active teenagers to look after, it seemed as though we were constantly chauffeuring someone. A few weeks of competing with the radio and a van full of chatter convinced us both to guard our sanity and make a change. So we experimented with asking personal questions as we ran the boys from one function to the next. Most of them loved this attention. Some even began volunteering to come along just for the ride — and a chance to share their feelings.

Others weren't ready to be so open. They would evade our questions and goof off. But as time went by, we learned they were willing to participate in group discussions. In fact, they thrived on the attention of the group more than the personal one-on-one situations. We discovered kids often compete with one another to see who can come up with the best answer. Whether in one-on-one, or in group settings, children and teenagers will eventually respond to questions if they feel you have a genuine interest in their lives.

Another opportunity for families to spend time in meaningful dialogue is on the way home from church. Young kids are often bursting at the seams to share what they've learned in Sunday School. What a great occasion to discuss spiritual matters! Walking or driving home from church is when people often feel closest to the Lord. A sharing time should be part of the weekly church experience.

How does a family remain close when sons and daughters no longer live at home? Perhaps an adult child has gone off to college. This was the case when Melissa began her first year at Gordon College in Wenham, Massachusetts. I (David) really missed our breakfast discussions. Because of the many miles between us, it was important to find an alternative to our father/daughter meetings. The logical solution was the telephone.

Just like the advertisements say, with a phone you can reach out and touch somebody. However, I didn't call Melissa without forethought. Before dialing her number, I worked through the questions I wanted to ask. I wanted to make sure as much as possible was covered in our conversation.

Often when people talk on the phone, they're busy doing other things. I have been guilty of this in the past. A recovering workaholic, I had a habit of washing dishes or doing other small projects while talking on the phone. It kept me busy, and I felt like I was accomplishing several things at the same time.

However, the people I was talking to often had a different perspective. They would comment that they didn't feel like I was listening to them. They felt my mind was on something other than what they were saying. It was! Since then, I've come to the decision that if I'm talking to a loved one on the phone, I need to give that person my full attention. The interesting thing is that these conversations are now far more satisfying to me too.

I got into a bad pattern, but I'm changing. And most people need to be encouraged to think in terms of new patterns in spending time with their children. If the old habit is to turn on the radio once you start the car, make it a new pattern to work on meaningful conversation with the ones you love. If you haven't really found out how your kids are doing, start today!

Chapter Five Discussions Questions

1. How good were your parents at finding out how you were doing mentally, physically, socially, and spiritually? What communication patterns did you learn from them that should be copied? Which should be discarded?

2. Do you wish someone would still encourage you to keep growing mentally, physically, socially, and spiritually? What can you do about this?

3. Give four reasons why it might be best for a parent to try to get away from the house to have a good talk with a child.
   a.

   b.

   c.

   d.

4. When your child responds honestly to questions, is your normal response to listen empathetically or to react? Why?

5. Are your children comfortable asking you questions? How can you encourage this capacity in them?

6. How might you relate better to other members of the family on the way home from church?

7. On a scale of 1 to 10 (10 being best) rate yourself on how well you make use of other times when you are in the car with your children.

Chapter 6

Asking Questions of People Jesus Sends Our Way

How would you feel if your wife called you at work and asked, "Honey, could you come home a little early tonight? We're having company over for dinner."

Perhaps that's not uncommon. Your wife enjoys having people over—often she invites the neighbors, a friend from the church, or your in-laws. So, you casually respond, "Sounds fine. Who's coming?"

Her answer is unexpected. Your jaw drops a bit. Did you hear correctly? Assuming you misunderstood, you half laughingly ask, "Who did you say? It almost sounded like..." She finishes your sentence. "Jesus.... I thought it would be nice to ask Him to be our dinner guest. We'll be eating with Him at 6:30. Please don't be late!"

Jesus as your dinner guest ... wouldn't that be exciting! He'd certainly be the center of attention. Given this opportunity, most people could think of any number of questions they would like to ask Jesus. Certainly these would get beyond "How are You, Jesus?" "Is that a new robe?" or "Ah, how's heaven?" Those who normally watch TV during dinner would hopefully have the sense to say, "Turn it off! How many times do we have the privilege of having Jesus here?"

What would it be like to participate in the household of Lazarus, Mary, and Martha whenever Jesus stayed at their home? Can you imagine their anticipation at having an entire evening to talk face-to-face with the miracle-working Christ? Sounds marvelous, doesn't it?

Do you know what? It's possible to experience all of this today. At least it is if we take our Lord's words in Matthew 25 at face value. In verses 35-40, the King says to those on His right, "I was a stranger and you invited Me in." The righteous then ask Him, "When did we see You a stranger and invite You in?" To this the King replies, "I tell you the truth, whatever you did for one of the least of these brothers of Mine, you did for Me."

It sounds like when we invite visitors into our homes, we do well to treat them as we would treat Jesus. This includes honoring them and maybe spending quality time asking them more questions than we would the average guest.

What else would change if we viewed each guest as Christ disguised in that person's form? The kind of topics we normally talk about might seem trivial. No longer would a large portion of the evening center on talk about our job promotion, the plans to put an addition on the house, or the exceptional feature on our new VCR. These trifles would quickly lose any significance.

If Jesus were our dinner guest, our focus would change. We'd be more interested in asking Him questions than in going on and on about ourselves. We'd want to learn as much about Him as we possibly could. And this should also be our attitude when we spend time with visitors. When we invite people into our homes, we should treat them as honored guests. According to Christ, when we've done that, it's the same as entertaining the Lord Himself.

The Mains household has had Jesus over for dinner many times. One way we participate in this miracle is through a fun family game built upon asking questions. We've played it together for years. The best setting is around the dinner table, but it can take place anywhere. It doesn't matter whether the guest is someone famous or simply a friend from school.

The way the game works is simple. Each family member takes a turn asking our guest a question. Before we begin, we explain, "We have a tradition we always stick to when someone visits here for the first time. We want to get to know you. So, we'll each ask you one question, and you have to answer everyone as honestly as you can." No one remembers how that last part about honesty got in there, but it tends to put the fear of God into people!

Seriously, our guests usually delight in such an opportunity. As they talk candidly about themselves, their eyes light up. They feel special because everyone around the table is listening enthusiastically to each of their responses.

No one knows what questions will be asked. The possibilities are endless, and family members constantly come up with new ones. They range from, "If you didn't have to worry about money and you could take a vacation anywhere in the world, where would you go, and why?" to "Tell me a favorite biblical character and how you relate to him or her." The object is to allow our guests to talk openly about themselves. As the conversation progresses, their answers reveal more and more about who they are. These evenings are always warm times of fellowship, and people often share touching personal stories.

A typical question we might ask is, "Name someone who had a positive influence on you as you were growing up, and how did he or she affect your life?" It's a simple question, and yet it's not something people often think about. Many times we see our guests mentally sorting through the back recesses of their minds before they speak. This silent inventory eventually produces a slight grin. When they finally answer, it's fascinating to hear the admirable ways others helped to mold them into the people they are.

Some other questions are:
— Who is someone you would really like to meet and why?
— What's a day you would love to relive if you could?
— What hobbies did you have both as a little kid and as a big kid?
— What personal dream do you hope will come true someday?
— What would you change about yourself if you could?
— When you were in the sixth grade, what girl/boy did you like and why?
— What's one of the good things about the church you grew up in?

As we mentioned in chapter 2, before too long you'll be able to tell the difference between a good question and a bad one. A question that's too hard to answer shouldn't be used again. For example, we learned it's not good to ask people, "Who has influenced your life the most?" Guests have trouble quickly choosing one most influential person. A better question is, "Name someone who influenced your life, anyone who comes to mind, and why was that person important to you." That's better. Guests can always respond because it doesn't pressure them to come up with one correct or perfect answer.

You can cover so many topics during this game. Personality traits are always interesting to me (Melissa). I'll ask, "How are you like your dad, and how are you like your mom? Then, which parent are you most like, and in what ways?" Many times visitors will say, "Well, I have my mom's outgoing mannerisms and my dad's creativity. But I'm most like Mom because. . . ." The answer helps me better understand our guest's personality.

An incredible bonding takes place during these times together. People love to talk about themselves, and having the opportunity to do so gives them the feeling we value them highly.

Many times, when thinking up my question, I (David) try to consider what Jesus might ask our guest. Perhaps Christ would inquire, "What's a spiritual victory you've known in your life recently?" or "What are some of the struggles you're facing right now?" So, on Jesus' behalf, I just ask the question for Him. If hard-pressed, I can always use my old favorite, "How are you doing spiritually?"

Often someone will ask, "How did you

become a Christian?" The stories are always different. Nevertheless, it's so thrilling to hear people talk about their spiritual journeys! And listening to others share their life experiences helps us appreciate the amazing way God works.

Sometimes our guests are non-Christians. During those visits I'll usually explain, "You know, I'm a minister, and spiritual things are important to me. Is that an interest of yours at all?" Surprisingly, people are quite open and honest when they answer. Maybe they'll tell me they really aren't interested in God or the church. If I ask them why they feel this way, they might respond, "I've had bad church experiences, and I guess I'm bitter about the way I was treated." That's OK. I'm just glad they opened up! Now I'm able to be more sensitive to their hurts and needs.

Being a writer, my wife, Karen, frequently asks, "Tell me what books you've read lately," or "What is one of your all-time favorite books?" If they aren't readers, she'll ask them, "What's a film or video you've enjoyed watching, and why?"

These evenings are filled with joy. We laugh hysterically whenever people share crazy things that happened to them. "What was an embarrassing moment you had when you were in school?" A question like that almost always provokes an enjoyable answer!

As the conversation continues, we all construct a better picture of who our guest is. It's like the pieces of a jigsaw puzzle coming together. Whether we've shared in their laughter or their tears, the time has been most meaningful. By the close of our discussion, we've made a new friend. Our family has honored our guest, and because of that, the person leaves our home feeling like he or she also has made several new friends.

During these meals, we attempt to have a mind-set that says, "We want to practice the Lord's presence by seeing through His eyes and hearing with His ears. We treat our guests just like we would treat Jesus . . . with honor, respect, and as someone of great importance. That's because we know the secret that Christ is here with us in disguise."

What a wonderful privilege to live in the reality of this supernatural element! It transforms a common meal into an experience with eternal ramifications.

Chapter Six Discussion Questions

1. Were you ever a dinner guest somewhere, but felt nobody cared if you were there or not? Why was this?

2. Are there other Bible verses which affirm that you can minister to Christ by reaching out to someone else? (Add these to the ones suggested on page 72.)

3. When extending any kind of Christian love to others, have you ever experienced the feeling that you were ministering to Jesus Himself? If so, what was this like?

4. Name someone you might invite to your home in order to know firsthand the joy of ministering to Christ.

5. How elaborate should a meal served for Christ be to feel you have adequately honored Him?

6. A sincere dinner prayer can make it easier for guests to sense the Lord's presence around a table. Give an example of the kind of table prayer that does the exact opposite.

7. When a meal is served at the church, what factors contribute to whether or not people will interact in a meaningful way?

Write out five questions you might ask a dinner guest.

1.

2.

3.

4.

5.

Passages about true ministry having more than just a human dimension.

Matthew 25:31-46
Hebrews 13:2
Matthew 10:40-42
Genesis 18:1-15
Hebrews 6:10

Chapter 7

How Questions Help in a Setting of Polarization

Think about how many people today feel misunderstood. You see them filled with intense anger. After years of bottling up negative emotions, they have become bitter toward others and alienated from society. Why?

Our world is changing in many ways. No longer do we have a common code of ethics. What you think is right may be the opposite of what your neighbor believes. Too often, this results in polarization.

Polarization—don't let that word intimidate you! It comes from polarity, which means to be opposite or contradicting. Like the magnetic poles, one attracts and the other repels. You can force the extremes together, but as soon as the pressure is removed, they push apart again.

Look, for example, at the Middle East. The Arab-Jew polarity is obvious. It's almost impossible to bring these two groups together. They have such a long history of misunderstanding, bitterness, and retaliation that the only way they know how to relate is through accusations and violence. Reconciliation seems impossible.

Unfortunately, many people relate the same way when dealing with differences. When discussing issues with those who have opposite viewpoints, they tend to get angry, defensive, and critical. How do we break the stalemate? In a polarized society where people feel misunderstood, alienated, or threatened, the simple skill of learning to ask good questions can bring about reconciliation.

What are some of the opposing issues involving the church? An obvious one is the Pro-Life/Pro-Choice conflict. In the media you hear daily reports about the huge differences between these positions. Each side has strong convictions. And each side also has a growing resentment against what the opposition holds so dear.

Other examples include the breach between Gay Rights activists and the church's conservative majority, where each side attacks the other. We find battles going on between the sexes — men and women consistently misunderstand and hurt one another. Racism still exists. How sad to have to admit this. There's the generation gap, with older and younger people having difficulty understanding each other's opinions about music, clothing, money, and morality. Often polarization occurs in political issues as candidates attempt to magnify party differences. We don't have to search long to find polarities.

The word *reconciliation* means to bring opposing parties together. That skill needs to be learned. And again, the ability to ask good questions and then listen carefully to the responses given can help reconcile polarities.

In the church, we must learn to deal more appropriately with groups having opposing viewpoints. The bad news is most churches aren't very good at asking questions and then listening closely to the answers given. They're more likely to shout, "Shut up and hear our opinion! You need to understand that we're right!"

But, there's also some good news! It's not hard to learn to ask good questions and listen empathetically. And the benefits far outweigh the minimal effort involved!

In Matthew 5:9, Jesus says, "Blessed are the peacemakers, for they will be called sons of God." We need to follow Christ's example and work to bring about reconciliation between people, even if we can't reconcile their ideas. This is not a typical mind-set in the church. So we need to train ourselves to think, "I may not agree with this person, but can I learn to better understand where he's coming from? If I show understanding, maybe I can eventually share Christ's love. At least I can pursue peace rather than war."

In John 4, Christ sets an example for us to follow by talking with a Samaritan woman.

In order to understand the significance of this act, it's important to realize the historical polarization between Samaritans and Jews.

Back in the Old Testament, there were twelve tribes of Israel. After Solomon's reign, the ten northern tribes split off from the two southern neighboring tribes. They began serving idols, and eventually built their own place of worship in their capital city, Samaria. The two nations, Northern Israel and Southern Judah, crowned different kings and eventually ended up fighting each other.

The northern tribes were conquered first. The victorious Assyrians deported many captives to other countries and imported foreigners to Israel, forcing those remaining to intermarry. To the Southern Jews, these people became half-breeds. The tribes of the north lost their identity and became "The Ten Lost Tribes of Israel."

By the time of Christ, the "true" Jews wanted nothing to do with these Samaritans. They held them in contempt. These people were dogs. Jews wouldn't talk to them or travel through their territory. Like Jews and Arabs today, everyone knew they didn't get along.

But in this John 4 passage Jesus deals radically with these issues. He travels through Samaria instead of around it. Tired from His journey, our Lord stops at a well to rest. Along comes a Samaritan woman to draw water. We won't even go into the significance of Jesus talking to a *woman*. Suffice it to say, He went against the norm again. But notice how He initiates a conversation with this woman by making a simple inquiry, "May I have a drink?"

The question was appropriate. They were at a well and He was thirsty. As you read, you'll see how Jesus shows respect and compassion for this woman. He doesn't tell her that as a Jew He disagrees with everything she represents. He looks past their differences and begins a constructive conversation by asking a simple question.

The woman seems a bit startled. She isn't used to being spoken to by a man, and certainly not by a Jew. Yet this simple question begins a wonderful conversation which soon brings reconciliation between the Samaritan woman and her Lord. Her life is changed, and she becomes an incredible evangelist! Because of her witness, all sorts of people from her city become a part of Christ's kingdom!

Who are the Samaritans in our society? While reading this chapter, perhaps someone came to mind with whom you differ so much that the thought of understanding each other seems impossible.

How do you gain experience in learning the reconciliation process? The first step is simply to pick someone you have a tough time relating to. Here is a list of the kinds of people who may differ from you. See if you can think of specific individuals who might fit some of these categories.

A person who . . .
— doesn't share your faith in Christ
— is at least fifteen–twenty years older or younger than you
— represents a different nationality
— is a family member you often argue with
— worships at another church
— has different values than you have
— you usually disagree with
— you had a problem with in the past
— you haven't seen for a long time
— is of a different religion altogether
— thinks differently than you do about the role of men and women in the church

When I (David) went through this list, I chose the category of someone who is decidedly younger than myself. I'm in my mid-fifties and the little girl I picked is almost fifty years my junior. She is a darling child who spends a lot of time in our home. She also has limitless energy and loves to talk!

Unfortunately, I don't know much about the things that are important to her. But I see that in order to relate to her, I'm going to have to work at better understanding her world. It's been a long time since I've watched "Mr. Roger's Neighborhood." Maybe that's a show I'll have to get back in touch with, because she likes it. Some of our conversations will probably revolve around Play-Doh, or Big Bird, Ernie, and Bert. These are matters I seldom spend time thinking about. But if I want to make the friendship a good one, these common ties will enable me to better understand who this child is.

No matter how huge the differences are between people, they can start to come together if one party asks, "How do I learn more about this person's world? And what questions can I ask that will help me better understand where she (he) is coming from?"

While reading over the categories listed earlier, did someone specific come to mind? How are you going to draw closer to that person despite your differences? The first step is to make a conscious effort to get beyond debates and arguments. Don't concentrate on rehearsing your convictions. Instead think, "How can I better understand who this person is? And how can I begin to relate in a way that will bring about reconciliation?"

If you establish these questions in your mind before your conversations, it will be natural to ask questions that could ultimately lead to the healing of a polarized relationship.

Chapter Seven Discussion Questions

1. What polarizations in our society are you most aware of?

2. What reaction can you expect when you argue with someone about your differences?

3. Summarize what you understand the main point of chapter 7 to be.

4. Is it a "copout" to work at trying to understand the other person's position rather than attempting to convince him of yours? Why or why not?

5. If you were to be a true peacemaker, who might misunderstand and criticize you?

6. Have you filled the peacemaker role, even if reconciliation has not been forthcoming? Why or why not?

7. With the many polarizations that mark our society, generally speaking, has the church been more on the side of the problem or the solution? Explain your answer.

Write down names of individuals you know who fit these categories:

People who don't share my faith in Christ

People at least fifteen–twenty years older or younger than my age

People of a different nationality

People who are family members I often argue with

People who worship at a different church

People whose values differ from mine

People with whom I usually disagree

People I have had a problem with in the past

People I haven't seen for a long time

People of a different religion altogether

People who think differently than I do about the role of men and women in the church

Questions to Ask Non-Christians

"My car broke down," you explain to a scruffy auto mechanic. "What's wrong with it?" he retorts. That's one question you never quite know how to answer.

"Um . . . well . . . it just made some funny noises and quit."

He gives you a disgruntled look and peers under the hood. Just when you think he'll never find the problem, he pops up and explains the situation. You listen intently.

"It looks like your distributor cap came off the housing and the oil's spilled over into the valve caps. Notice your valves? They're charred. Besides that, bud, your master cylinder's leakin' and the differential's. . . ."

Every mechanical muscle in your brain strains to track with what he's saying. You haven't missed a word, but already he's lost you! You notice yourself unconsciously nodding your head, "Uh huh. . . ."

Why did you make that little grunt of affirmation? You don't have any idea where the whatchamijigger is or how it connects to the thingamabob! When it's all over, your bottom line is always the same: "How much will it cost?" and "When do you think it will be ready?"

I (David) have been in this predicament quite a few times. When having car repairs explained to me, I end up just nodding my head. The problem is, I don't learn anything. I leave the shop knowing as little as when I came in.

When speaking about spiritual matters with nonbelievers, the Christian is usually the expert. If I (David) were to explain spiritual things the way the mechanic does, people would simply nod their heads and agree. But that doesn't mean they'd understand any-thing.

So, I make it a rule to ask questions as much as possible when I talk to others about Christ. This has been a good technique, be-cause it keeps me from falsely assuming peo-ple are following what I'm saying. Asking questions allows me to probe their under-standing and find out where they're coming from. This way, if they're having trouble fol-lowing me, I'll know precisely where I've lost them.

How do you know whether someone is interested in talking about spiritual things or is even ready to accept Christ? Often people drop hints during a conversation. They'll make statements like, "You know, someone in my family just became one of those born-again Christians" or "I have a real problem in my life, and I need help." I let them explain their situation. Then, through questions, I begin directing the conversation toward Christ.

There are five basic questions I come back to again and again. Each one narrows the focus a little more. Once the matter of spiritual things has come up, my first question is, **"Suppose you were to become a Christian, how do you see that changing the way you live?"** Answers range from, "I guess I would need to start going to church" to, "I'm living with my girlfriend, and I'm sure I'd have to either move out of her apartment or get married" to, "I'd need to stop cussing!"

After listening to the person's answer, I might comment that what he or she has said falls in line with what Jesus taught. Christ said in order to follow Him we must love God with all our hearts. He also told us to love our neighbors as we love ourselves. "So," I say, "if you're not going to church, you're probably not loving God the way you should; likewise, if you're using His name in vain, you will want to begin speaking it in a more reverent fashion," or, "I agree, you're not really treating your girlfriend in a way that honors her."

I explain, "If you don't want to love God and you don't want to love people, then you don't want to be a Christian, because that's how you're supposed to live." I like to establish up front what Christ's expectations are of a person who says yes to Him.

The second question is, **"Do you think you've fallen short of this standard of loving God and loving others?"** Almost always people answer, "Yes. I'm selfish, I know I am . . . I don't love God or people the way I should." I explain to them that failing to meet this standard is what Scripture calls sin. It's like shooting at a target and missing it. One biblical definition of sin is "to miss the mark."

This person's sin has contributed to the pain that surrounds us. What a wonderful world it would be if everyone loved God and loved people the way the Creator intended. Society would be beautiful if everyone copied the lifestyle of Christ's love for His Father, and for His brothers and sisters. But the Bible makes it plain that all have fallen short of His example.

I then ask my third question, **"Can you solve this problem without God's help? Is it possible on your own to forgive your past sins, and then start living the new way of loving both God and people?"** Only once have I had someone respond, "I think I can." At that point we went to passages in Scripture to see what the Bible says.

Usually I don't open the Bible or quote passages early in the conversation. Scripture is intimidating to non-Christians. It's like me and the auto repairman—no matter what I read, the other guy just nods his head and says, "Uh-huh." In my experience of leading people to the Lord, I've found asking questions and listening carefully to the answers they give is most effective, though my Bible is always close by to turn to at the appropriate time.

Typically, however, people realize they need God's help if there is to be a true change in their lives. The common response is, "I don't believe I can solve the problem of sin on my own. I have a history of failure."

As you can see, each question builds on the previous one. They're simple, not abrasive or intimidating, yet their impact is profound! Used with sensitivity, these questions enable non-Christians to search their hearts and realize their needs.

Only two questions are left, and they're the best ones of all! The fourth is, **"If you can't solve your problem, do you think Jesus can solve it for you?"** When the answer I get is, "Yes," I'll say, "Tell me why you think He can." Often at this point, a person will talk about how a grandparent took her to Sunday School when she was a child. There she learned that Jesus was the example of how we should live, that He can forgive our sins, and that even today the Spirit of the risen Christ can live inside us.

By further probing, I make sure my friend understands why Christ died on the cross, and also the importance of the Resurrection. If clarification is needed, I'll slowly explain everything over again. Once my friend understands how Jesus can solve his or her problem of sin, I move on to my final inquiry.

Let me insert this caution: When people don't want to pursue the subject further, they'll say things like, "I think we've been on this topic long enough now," or "Let's talk about something else." That's fine. Don't make it a negative experience by forcing the issue. Perhaps he won't become a Christian just then, but you certainly have allowed him to begin processing where he is spiritually. God's timing is perfect!

If the individual continues to show interest, however, I move on to number five. This is a marvelous question, and I love asking it! **"If you believe Jesus can solve your problem, when do you think would be a good time to ask Him to do that?"** Many Christian people get stuck here in their evangelizing. They realize the other party is open to making a decision, but they aren't sure how to bring about closure. This last question is an incredible help.

But allow the person to decide how to answer it. Don't go by your own agenda or tell someone the best time for him or her is right now. It's not your decision. I've had people answer, "I need a couple of days to think about it." "OK," I respond. "I'll call you in three days." One man told me, "I'm going on the 50-Day Spiritual Adventure. After I finish that, I may want to ask Jesus to save me." "That's fine," I said. "I'll contact you then." After fifty days I called him, and he asked Jesus to be his Lord and Savior. Now he's still going strong.

Most people answer, "I think right now would be a good time to ask for His help." "Wonderful!" I respond. "Let me take you to the place where I first met Jesus. It's called Calvary. We'll go there in prayer. That way, when you see Jesus in your mind, He'll be on the cross. We know, of course, He's risen from the dead. But I want you to be reminded of how He had to die so you could experience this miracle."

As we pray together, I ask the person to picture himself or herself kneeling before the cross. "Look up to Jesus now," I suggest. "Pray, 'Jesus, I haven't lived as I should. I can't solve my problems, but I believe You can. You shed Your blood so I could be forgiven. That's what I want. Wash me clean of all my wrongdoing. Come into me by Your Holy Spirit and begin the work of teaching me how to live Your new and better way!' "

Up until this point, there isn't usually a lot of emotion. But all of a sudden, when the person starts talking to Jesus, eyes fill up with tears, and the man or woman will begin crying. That's because a supernatural encounter takes place. There at the cross, salvation is made real to another seeker.

These five questions help me understand people's needs and hurts. By asking them I've learned to communicate the profound message of Christ in a simple way. Unlike the auto mechanic who confuses his customers as soon as he starts talking, it's fulfilling to know that people didn't just grunt an affirmation to what I've said. And how wonderful to walk them down the path that leads to Jesus Himself.

Chapter Eight Discussion Questions

1.   Have you ever been present when some-
     one became a new Christian? Tell what
     you observed.

2.   Which of the five key questions in chapter
     8 was the most helpful to you and why?
     (a) Suppose you were to become a Chris-
         tian, how do you see that changing the
         way you live?
     (b) Do you think you've fallen short of this
         standard of loving God and loving
         others?
     (c) Can you solve this problem without
         God's help? Is it possible on your own
         to forgive your past sins, and then start
         living the new way of loving both God
         and people?
     (d) If you can't solve your problem, do you
         think Jesus can solve it for you?
     (e) If you believe Jesus can solve your
         problem, when do you think would be a
         good time to ask Him to do that?

3. In what specific ways can using questions benefit a Christian in his/her witness for Christ?

4. What advantages are there for a non-Christian when the person witnessing makes use of questions?

5. How should you respond if the person to whom you are witnessing asks a question which diverts from the direction you have established?

6. Did Christ push people to make an immediate commitment? Illustrate your answer from an incident in Scripture.

7. If questions had seldom been used in your schooling, would you have learned more or less? Why?

Chapter 9

More Ways Asking Questions Can Benefit the Church

"Where are you?" That's a question God asks Adam early in the Old Testament. Just a bit later the Lord asks Cain, "Why is your face downcast?"

Actually, the Scriptures are filled with God asking questions. "Abraham, why did Sarah laugh?" "Jacob, what is your name?" "Moses, what is that in your hand?" "Elijah, what are you doing here?" "Isaiah, whom shall I send?"

When you get to the New Testament you realize Jesus, a most effective communicator, was skilled at asking good questions. He challenged people to think through what He taught. He didn't just say, "OK, guys. Here's the scoop. . . . Get it! Got it? Good."

Instead, Christ made sure people processed the ideas He presented. Feedback helped Him understand the heart and soul of the people to whom He was ministering. Here is a small sampling of the many questions we hear Christ ask in the Gospel:

"Which is easier: to say, 'Your sins are forgiven,' or to say, 'Get up and walk'?"

"Can you make the guests of the bridegroom fast while he is with them?"

"If you love those who love you, what credit is that to you?"

"Can a blind man lead a blind man?"

"Where is your faith?"

"What is your name?"

"Who touched Me?"

"Who do the crowds say I am?"

"What is written in the Law?"

"Why are you sleeping?"

"What are you discussing together as you walk along?"

"Why are you troubled, and why do doubts rise in your minds?"

"Simon son of John, do you truly love Me more than these?"

Jesus knew the importance of a two-way exchange. Not only did He ask good questions, He was comfortable being questioned by others as well. Too often we view Christ solely as a preacher and in a setting where it would be out of place for anyone to interrupt Him. But much of the time Jesus ministered outside, where the rules were quite different from a contemporary worship service.

Many of the communication techniques Jesus used involved questions. His purpose was to change lives. He asked questions to learn whether this was happening. When do we in the church use questions to be sure our message has been clearly understood?

The truth is, we could improve in this area. Too often when people leave a church service, they smile, shake the pastor's hand, and comment, "Good sermon." And that's that. But does the average pastor really know if his message was effective? Was his communication clear? Did his congregation learn anything? Will lives be changed? It's extremely difficult to minister to people's needs without good feedback. Maybe the church needs to rediscover Christ's practice of asking questions in order to be more effective in its ministry.

What are some simple ways congregations could incorporate the use of questions? One obvious method would be through interviews. Too often churches rely on preaching when an interview could be more effective. But be aware that a good interview, like a good sermon, requires work. It takes time to come up with just the right questions.

Never do an interview without first getting to know the person involved. Maybe he or she has written a book you can read. If the individual is a missionary, have dinner together and find out what is exciting about his or her work. What questions need to be asked for the congregation to identify with this person's heartbeat? Remember, statistics aren't as interesting as personal stories. "How many people have come to the Lord?"

might be replaced with, "Tell us the story of one person who's come to the Lord." Again, a good interview is hard work. You are the key to this person living in the hearts of the congregation.

During the interview, allow the conversation to be as natural as possible. If the mood of an answer is amusing, don't fight it! Laughter is a wonderful gift that keeps people involved with the basic presentation. Allow your guests to express themselves freely while you, the interviewer, keep the topic focused.

A good interview captures the intimacy of a private conversation while allowing a large group to listen in. Suppose a church wants to inform parents of the peer pressure high school students face. Which would the congregation be more likely to identify with, a minister preaching on the topic or an interview with several students themselves? Wouldn't it be much more powerful to listen to two or three students answer questions and openly share the pressures they feel as Christians today?

Here's another example. A minister wants to preach about living out your faith at work. Certainly he could tell how to do this in a sermon. But wouldn't it be powerful to interview a salesman, a shop foreman, and an account executive? "You say you feel good about living out your faith at work. Why do you feel this way?" "Help us understand some of the ways you've done this." "What are a few of the difficulties you've faced?" "What Scriptures are especially meaningful to you in this area?" Questions like these allow the topic to be exciting, and the method has a way of drawing people in. The congregation will listen even more intently than usual.

Another benefit of the interview format is that it allows the guest to be at ease, because someone else is responsible for coming up with good questions and directing the conversation. People who aren't used to public speaking can experience enormous pressure and fear. The interview puts the responsibility on the person asking the questions and allows the guest to be himself.

If Jesus were to visit our contemporary scene, it's likely He'd do well on the interview-formatted talk shows. Barbara Walters, Oprah, and Donahue would all be trying to get Him as a guest. How do you think Jesus would respond? Would He tell them, "I don't do interviews, I only preach"? Or would He be their guest and discuss His cares and concerns for our troubled world? We believe He'd be very comfortable communicating this way.

Don't forget that Christ was also a fantastic debater. The Pharisees and Sadducees constantly interrupted Jesus to ask Him pointed questions. Look at His responses. Did He say, "It's not nice for you to interrupt Me when I'm talking," or did He answer them?

Often Jesus responded to questions by asking another or by turning the focus to the real problem at hand. He wasn't afraid of open debate; in fact, He seemed to thrive on it. I (David) believe the church could be more effective if it, like Christ, incorporated the use of debate and interviewing.

"Who do people say I am?" Jesus probed His disciples. Why did He ask this? He wanted feedback. In a sense, He was taking a survey. He wanted to know what people were saying about Him. Our Lord was also interested in what His disciples thought. Obviously, He recognized the importance of staying in touch with people's thoughts and feelings. And the primary way He accomplished this was through asking questions.

Surveys are a great way to find out people's opinions and interest areas. Have you ever been at a shopping center and had someone come up to you and say, "On behalf of the management, could I get you to answer a few questions?" The reason they do this is to get in touch with the consumer's wants and needs. They're out to please their customers by offering them the best products or services possible. Churches would benefit from using surveys too.

Why shouldn't a minister put in the church bulletin, "I'm considering speaking on the following topics. Which one would be most interesting and helpful to you? Please choose, and then place this survey in the box at the back of the chapel."

☐ An in-depth study of Romans
☐ How to manage stress
☐ Guidelines for family television and VCR viewing

A lot of people would be interested in either learning how to manage stress or figuring out guidelines for TV viewing. The book study on Romans would probably get the least number of votes. However, if a pastor chooses a topic without input from his congregation, most likely Romans would be his first choice. So, surveys can use questions to help church leaders enhance their ministry.

Are Sunday School class members retaining anything? Do people "turn off" as soon as the sermon begins, or are they learning? The tool of testing is a good way to find out. Testing is simply asking questions to learn if a given method is still effective. This could be easily done in the Sunday School class or through an insert in the church bulletin.

When my husband and I (Melissa) began teaching youth, we assumed the group had a good knowledge of the Scriptures. However, after playing a game of Bible trivia, we found they hadn't retained even the basics. The simple question, "Who was put in the lions' den?" brought either blank stares or responses like, "David?"

Obviously, we had a problem! These kids didn't know the Bible stories they should have learned as primaries. Yet, they were expected to live decidedly Christian lives. Since our children are vulnerable to the world's influences, the church ought to adopt the tool of testing to find out where new generations stand. Instead of worrying about who we might offend, we need to be concerned about whether we are teaching our offspring to defend themselves and make sound biblical decisions.

Testing doesn't always have to be in written form. During a youth lock-in we gathered the group in a small room and had them all sit on the floor to play a game. The rules were simple. The person with the ball rolled it to anyone he wanted. That person in turn had to tell one thing he knew about Jesus. We weren't expecting any great revelations to come out of this game, but it was a way to test the kids without having them feel like they were in school. The amazing thing was, the kids had a great time!

In fact, they didn't want to stop playing

and were begging for the ball to be rolled to them. Answers ranged from, "Jesus was a man" to "Jesus died on the cross to forgive our sins." One junior high boy, visiting for the first time, said, "He wasn't married, right?" This was fine. We supported him and affirmed that his answer was correct. At the same time, it helped us understand his Bible knowledge.

Perhaps the church isn't as strong as it thinks it is in its teaching. Testing can help us find out. Questions don't have to be threatening; simple ones like, "How have you applied what you've learned over the last month?" or "What was the main point of today's sermon?" clarify how effective the teaching has been.

All through the Bible, God asked questions. Christ posed questions throughout His ministry. Christians need to understand that the church can be more effective if it copies this example and becomes more comfortable asking questions too.

But the process probably won't get very far if the average person in the pew doesn't start working right away at getting beyond "How are you?"

Chapter Nine Discussion Questions

1. Do you think pastors/priests assume their people are more biblically literate than they really are?

2. What level of accurate feedback do you feel your minister gets as to the effectiveness of his ministry?

3. If a pastor wanted to test the congregation (no grades) as to how much was learned during a major preaching series, would you support this? Why or why not?

4. Are you open to the church staff using surveys to find out the thoughts of the congregation on various topics?

5.   Would the use of debate in a young adult
     Sunday School class make its members
     more or less secure in their faith over the
     long haul? Why?

6.   Do you have an opinion as to why the
     church has been relatively slow to make
     use of the technique of asking questions?

7.   What is the connection between you get-
     ting beyond "How are you?" and the
     church making greater use of questions?

8.   You are to interview your pastor who is re-
     tiring. Write down five good questions you
     might ask about his years of faithful
     service.

9. The church music committee has asked you to write a report on the impact of the music program on junior high students. You decide to interview a group of three or four of them. Write down five helpful questions you might ask.

10. As you read Scripture, begin writing down references you discover where God makes use of questions. Also write down references you come across where Christ makes use of questions during His ministry.

Matthew   *Mark*   *Luke*   *John*

CPSIA information can be obtained
at www.ICGtesting.com
Printed in the USA
LVOW10s2200250118
563789LV00001B/34/P